# Monday Messages

*Reflections on Life, Leadership,
and Learning in Our Schools*

LOU ANTONETTI

**BALBOA**.
PRESS
A DIVISION OF HAY HOUSE

Balboa Press books may be ordered through booksellers or by contacting:

Balboa Press
A Division of Hay House
1663 Liberty Drive
Bloomington, IN 47403
www.balboapress.com
1 (877) 407-4847

Because of the dynamic nature of the Internet, any web addresses or
links contained in this book may have changed since publication and
may no longer be valid. The views expressed in this work are solely those
of the author and do not necessarily reflect the views of the publisher,
and the publisher hereby disclaims any responsibility for them.

The author of this book does not dispense medical advice or prescribe the use
of any technique as a form of treatment for physical, emotional, or medical
problems without the advice of a physician, either directly or indirectly. The
intent of the author is only to offer information of a general nature to help
you in your quest for emotional and spiritual well-being. In the event you use
any of the information in this book for yourself, which is your constitutional
right, the author and the publisher assume no responsibility for your actions.

Any people depicted in stock imagery provided by Thinkstock are
models, and such images are being used for illustrative purposes only.
Certain stock imagery © Thinkstock.

Printed in the United States of America.

ISBN: 978-1-4525-9604-4 (sc)
ISBN: 978-1-4525-9603-7 (e)

Library of Congress Control Number: 2014906731

Balboa Press rev. date: 07/11/2014

This book is dedicated to my father who was a teacher, coach and true "family man."

I am fortunate to have had your positive influence on my life for 21 years and know that you continue to guide me.

# Introduction

As we go through life it is important to be aware of our decisions and actions. Most people will go through life never being told how they can improve themselves, either personally or professionally. Many of us don't see ourselves for what we are or what we represent. It is important for all of us to reflect on our behavior and decision-making on a daily basis. Sometimes we get so caught up in our thinking that we never get to *think about how we think*. By taking a look in your "mental mirror" at the end of each day, you will be able to reflect upon your decisions to see yourself for what you really are. If I ask you to look in the mirror and tell me what you see, you would probably say that you are a person who needs to lose weight, have better hair, tone up or who should be taller. All we see on TV are infomercials showing us how to improve ourselves physically since that is the first thing people see. This represents the shallow society that we have become. Almost 100% of those who stand in front of a mirror will never say that they need to have a more positive attitude, be more patient, complain less or be less ego-driven. Do not judge your OWN book by its cover! These are things that, during a busy day, often go unnoticed and won't be addressed, and yet will affect the perception others have of you along the way. What better way to have a positive influence on students than by working on their ability to reflect on their behavior at a young age. The "being a legend in your own mind" thinking will diminish once you step out of your mental bubble to see how your attitudes impact others.

We run the rat race of life sometimes never knowing where our stress is coming from. We try to eliminate stressful things one by one or learn how to cope with them. Fact is, we are not solving our problems, we are only alleviating them temporarily. So when I ask you what do you see? Seeing is the result of being aware and is a much deeper sense than what meets the eye. Seeing and being aware of yourself and your surroundings will greatly improve the way you look at yourself and life in general. It is amazing to see the number of people who have total disregard for the way they act which negatively impacts our day. Such people should be the first ones to read this book, but unfortunately may be too stubborn to admit they can improve themselves. Improving yourself is more than just improving in the eyes of others, it's being able to put your head on the pillow each night, knowing that you are living according to the "aware" code. Being aware is not just taking note of what is going on around you, it is processing it and trying to understand why things are happening. Too many people take things for granted and don't appreciate what they have or what's happening until it's gone. We have so many interactions throughout life, which is why it's important to be aware of them and to learn from others as much as ourselves.

I myself have a difficult time letting go of interactions and conversations. When I say "letting go" I mean that I don't treat each one as just another interaction. By being aware, listening to people's words and understanding their actions, life becomes much more interesting. For instance, you will hear rookie professional athletes speak of how the game is extremely fast when they first enter the league. After they gain experience and become aware of their place in the moment, time seems to slow down. This allows them to perform at a higher level. Well, it's the same in life. When we are babies and children we run wildly about with reckless abandon not taking too much stock in what others do or say. We never take things personally because young minds are rarely focused enough to understand people's behavior. As we get older and wiser, certain things become more important in life and we should be able to focus on what makes us happy along with who makes us happy. The mind is a funny thing, and some people's minds mature slower than others. This is why I believe that the divorce rate in the United States is so high. People get married at a young age, might have children, then eventually realize that what they have isn't making them happy. Societal norms tell you that marriage and children are the true path to happiness but that is not true for everyone. As you become more aware of yourself you may realize that the person you married really isn't the one for you. You did not "see" this way back when because you weren't aware and "the game" did not slow down enough for you to see it developing in such a way.

I must emphasize that it's important for people to live their lives at a pace that is comfortable for them, not at the pace society expects. Too many of us conform at an early age and keep the trend alive, always being afraid to buck the system. I give those who go against the grain a lot of credit. They know what they want and they don't feel the need to be "closet competitive" to achieve happiness. We see many things in life that we think we SHOULD have, but fail to ask, do we really need them to be happy? And after we buy all those things we SHOULD have, then where does that leave us in the end? Are we any more aware of who we really are, or did we just satisfy the preconceived notion that since others have it I need it too. Basically, being aware is not judging others, it is being honest with yourself. If you are not honest with yourself then it is impossible to be so with people you interact with. People say that I live my life like an open book and am too open. I say, what do I have to hide? I am not ashamed of what I do and if I am ashamed of something I will do my best to correct it. There is no room in life for toxic behavior which is why we should not tolerate it from ourselves or others.

The main component of life that you need to leave at the door is your ego. Without an ego the vision of yourself and others becomes much clearer. It is impossible to be aware while harboring an ego. Egos cloud thinking and make us behave in a way that is not true to our inner soul. The ego wall blocks people from relaxed, positive interactions. Ego-driven people will never be aware they are missing out on positive interaction because they are not aware from the start. Emotions are a tough thing to handle, but the best leaders of organizations and in life are able to keep their egos and emotions in check.

The main purpose of this book is to capture different areas of life that we all can improve upon. Each day provides us with an opportunity to write another chapter in our book. The book we write for ourselves is based on our daily decisions. If only people could flip back to previous chapters to see how they behaved or reacted. Only then would they be aware of what they were, what they are and ultimately be aware of how their present actions are determining their future. Once you are aware, you will feel that you have taken a step back from the world and are observing from the outside. It is a surreal experience to witness the behavior of others in a way they themselves cannot comprehend in the moment.

A positive culture in school is so important, because without one, the negativity will flow throughout the halls of a building. So please use this book not only as an opportunity to improve your life but as a way to cultivate positive change in students and colleagues in your schools. It is my hope that this book can be used as a weekly reminder for students, teachers, administrators, various school personnel and coaches to reflect upon their daily purpose and how they are affecting people's lives. The goal is not only to help students reach their potential academically, but to help them build solid character before they enter the game of life. Please feel free to use these messages in your classroom to improve the character of students, which in turn may result in better outcomes both inside and outside of your school.

# Week 1

As I was rocking my daughter to sleep I couldn't stop thinking about how much she trusts me (and mommy!) to do right by her. The trust is something that is felt without words. The actions and consistency with which we exhibit care are something that is invaluable. She trusts that we will not let her fall and that no matter what position we hold her in, playing or sleeping, she trusts that we will keep her safe. She knows deep down inside that as she falls asleep on my lap or shoulder that she will wake up in a safe place.

Trust is something that builds bonds and makes teams & families stronger. Once somebody lies, even once, that bond is broken and sometimes irreparable. As you go through your daily obligations, let's remember that your actions define who you are. When teaching your students please remember that your consistent care and positive demeanor are felt by your classes. The level of trust you establish with your students can make or break your year. Once they know that you want them to succeed and you will do whatever possible to make it happen, they will respect your methods for getting them there. There will be tough times along the way, where you will have to set someone straight. Resistance may be avoided if your approach with that student is appropriate and a high level of trust exists.

Why, as we get older, do we trust less and less while becoming more jaded with all that we witness in school and our personal lives? Why do some of us feel that our teacher evaluations won't have a teacher's best interest at heart? School building administrators should strive to make you trust the process and want you to succeed. They should use every opportunity and piece of evidence to put teachers in a positive light. Just as my daughter knows she is in a safe place, you should know that you are in a safe place wherever you are teaching. You should be able to trust that administrators will not let you fall and will provide whatever support you need along the way.

# Week 2

*"After a difficult day with the children," a young mother says, "I like to take the car and go for a drive; I like to have something in my hands I can control."*
-Lawrence P. Fitzgerald

Isn't it amazing that we seem to want relief from stress and always seem to think that planning better or having more control over a situation will banish that stress. Sometimes we have plans in our head and when detours occur, we tend to take them as unnecessary interruptions. Believe it or not there may be a plan for each one of us. If we let stubbornness and the need for control to get in the way, we may never open up our minds to what is actually occurring in our lives.

When a "monkey wrench" is thrown into people's plans, they tend to become negative and frustrated. We tell students to seize the moment, but when we are working or with our families, do we focus on seizing control or seizing the moment? It is extremely important to have a plan in life but remember to possess the flexibility that will allow you to seize opportunities when they arise.

Sometimes we push in the wrong direction and disrupt the natural flow of our day.

So as we approach our workdays, don't take interruptions as a sign of "losing control." We all walk through the doors each morning with an agenda. Don't let your plans steer you away from moments that may help you learn about yourself or allow somebody else to learn from you. For the most part students are curious, but we tend to take too many questions and some classroom distractions the wrong way. Note to all teachers: look forward to opportunities in your lessons that allow you to deviate from the plan a bit to provide a teachable moment. You may be giving students a piece of information they will never forget. Recognizing opportunities, whether they be in the classroom or in our personal lives, is something that can make each day go from good to great!

# Week 3

"*The greatest gift you can give another is the purity of your attention.*"

-Richard Moss M.D.

People take public speaking workshops and writing courses but you never hear of people wanting to learn more about the art of listening. Listening takes patience while also shifting the focus away from yourself. In a day and age when information and knowing the latest news are powerful tools, people tend to talk about what's going on and what they know to make themselves feel important in society. In meetings and dealing with parents as educators, remember that trying to communicate with someone who talks "at" you is impossible. The conversation should include exchanges that complement one another, not two people simply stating their viewpoints.

Productive listening is usually done by people who do not have an ego and who are willing to hear another person's point of view. Listening can only be done when you are at peace in your own mind. This allows you to focus your attention on the other person. A teacher who listens to students or colleagues at work makes them feel important as opposed to those trying to constantly prove how important or knowledgeable they think they are.

Lack of communication is the source of many problems in the world. It can cause problems with families and at work in your classes or amongst colleagues. If people listened more and spoke less they would be surprised by what they were missing. You won't learn everything at once but the pieces you take with you from various conversations will help you grow as a person and professional.

By the way, listening to the quiet times are helpful too. Pay attention to how often you have the radio on in the car or the TV on at home. This technology adds to the distractions that exist in our lives. Turn off the TV and read a book, stare out the window at the leaves falling from trees, just "listen" to the peace and quiet during early morning or night. The rat race of life can take you away from moments that will make your life more fulfilling. You will actually be able to "listen" to yourself which is the most important conversation you can have before you start or end each day.

This nursery rhyme says it all!

A wise old owl sat in an oak,

The more he heard, the less he spoke,

The less he spoke, the more he heard,

Why aren't we all like that wise old bird?

# Week 4

*"This typxwritxr is xxcxllxnt xxcxpt for onx kxy. The 25 othxr lxttxrs work finx; but just onx goof-off lousxs up thx wholx job."*

-William D. Ellis

This quote reminds me that little things can always affect the bigger picture. It is important to be detail-oriented in our position as educators. Being in the public view means that somebody is always watching, listening or focusing on our every action. When it comes to dealing with the details of our jobs, a certain standard of performance should guide us. As time goes by many people tend to become more and more comfortable with their current position. Try to always remember the fervor you possessed when you entered school as a first year teacher.

We are all here for a purpose and expect our students to perform at a high level day in and day out. Our purpose is to help students succeed, even when their home environment may be working against us. We need to constantly remind ourselves to have a purpose behind all that we do. Turning job obligations into a checklist makes them lose their meaning and students/parents can see right through this. For example, when it comes to making phone calls home for students (especially for those who are not doing well) let's remember to leave enough time for the student to recover from their decline. Make phone calls to parents with a purpose, not just to say a call was made.

If you follow up with parents, please make sure you are doing it because you want to not because you have to. Living / Working with a purpose MOST of the time is very different from doing it ALL of the time. Remember that our daily habits make us who we are!

# Week 5

> *"The trouble with not having a goal is that you can spend your life running up and down the field and never scoring."*
>
> -Bill Copeland

Having a vision allows us to see the possibilities of tomorrow within the realities of today. A vision motivates us to do what needs to be done. Many of us have the potential to do great things, but feel that life is endless and may wait for the "right time." There is no perfect time for things to happen, which is why we must seize each moment. Luck is having preparation meet opportunity. Many of us have opportunities but are too busy to capitalize on them. I firmly believe that we can create our own luck in life. I laugh when people tell others they are lucky to be where they are today. Without knowing the hard work and sacrifice that someone has endured, calling someone lucky is an insult.

New Year's resolutions drive many people's actions. Each resolution requires focus and this focus can be taken away from us when dealing with the rat race of life. Remember to keep your mind calm, no matter how stressful or frantic things are on the outside. The race does not have to take place inside of your head. Clear thoughts equal a clear vision for your future. Where your thoughts go, your actions will soon follow. If you want positive results you must instill in yourself the will to execute consistent positive actions.

A group of people with a common goal can be powerful. Maybe have your class or team develop resolutions as a means to motivate them. I know you may have expressed goals to your students, but have they been given the chance to define legitimate goals as a group? You will be surprised at who steps up and who reinforces your goals as the year progresses. Many people believing in achievement can become contagious!

# Week 6

*"All people should strive to learn before they die, what they are running from, and to, and why."*

-James Thurber

Helping others reach their true potential is something in which every leader should take pride. Whether you are leading a school district, school building, department, team, club, orchestra or class of students, you want everyone to experience success. This is only possible if you lengthen the leash! We tend to help others too much when wanting them to succeed. The one thing adversity teaches us is how to respond to situations that are out of our control. The only way to learn how to do this is for someone to give you the chance to fail. That's right.....BE GRATEFUL IF SOMEONE GIVES YOU THE CHANCE TO FAIL. When this occurs someone is indirectly saying that they trust you. If they don't encourage you to make decisions on your own, take risks or think of new ideas, they don't trust you and will keep the safeguards on to protect the good of the group.

Allowing someone to fail may actually translate into an opportunity for that person to succeed. The worst thing that can happen is that the person may learn from a mistake or it may spark a trusting relationship. By setting people up for success all the time you are taking the guesswork out of it and they are no more valuable than a puppet. By allowing them to be assertive they will grow as a person from the experience.

Protecting others and not allowing them to make decisions does not empower them and they may never buy into what you are trying to accomplish. Remember to give students and colleagues the opportunity to fail, they might even thank you for it. IF YOU ARE GOING TO ALLOW SOMEONE TO FALL, LET THEM FALL FORWARD!!!

# *Week 7*

*"Decide what your priorities are and how much time you'll spend on them. If you don't, someone else will."*
-Harvey Mackay

I am sure that when all of us decided to go into education, it wasn't to worry about test scores and how we would compare to our colleagues. We can tell how effective teachers are based on their history and stopping in a room for 3-5 minutes. The only thing, along with content knowledge, that gets good results throughout the year is a solid RELATIONSHIP with your students.

Some people think that data drives instruction but I feel that data is just a tool in the toolbox. What drives instruction are relationships that motivate kids to want to come to class and learn. All the data in the world is worthless if you don't have motivated teachers and students to influence change. We are in the people business that is driven by relationships not numbers. Numbers can support our decisions but relationships are what put them into effect. Show students their test scores for the quarter…..will that motivate them to perform better? Probably not if the relationship with the teacher, parents and school is not solid.

People who hide behind data, sometimes use it as a way to communicate because they are afraid, or can't have difficult conversations when needed. Relating to colleagues and students is what makes a school a great place to work in each day. By spewing data and achievement gaps you don't build trust. We all know that we will only go as far as the teachers who are in the "trenches" each day. If you don't feel supported in your relationship with building administration it may carry over to your students, negatively impacting your instruction. I know that most of us are willing to take risks in the classroom and that obstacles that may prevent you from implementing first class lessons should be removed when they arise. The data will speak for itself when students make it a priority to perform at a high level in your class.

# Week 8

*"Adversity causes some men to break, others to break records."*

-William Arthur Ward

I found it quite ironic that when the blizzard of 2013 hit the Northeast region, our school district was in the middle of budget talks. Rumors were starting to swirl around our district just as the snow whipped twice as fast. Our fiscal situation presented obstacles while the blizzard presented us with a lot of uncertainty along with the need to make sacrifices as we fought through it. When anticipating adversity the only thing we can do is prepare. Worrying will not relieve us from what is going on, it will only cloud our thinking. Think about it…What did we do when news of the blizzard was confirmed? Most people bought a shovel (if they didn't have one already), salt, food, gas and batteries. Not many people sat at home worrying, hoping that it wouldn't snow. They most likely gave it their best effort to prepare for the worst. It is always a good idea to have tools in your belt that will help you build towards a solid future.

My point here is that we need to make the best of a situation that is out of our control. If we sit around listening to other people, their negativity and spewing of rumors, we may not recognize opportunities that will allow us to deal with these external forces more appropriately. As people began to ask me my opinion on the whole budget situation I remained positive and did not worry about things that were out of my (our) control. Remember now and in the bigger scheme of life, to have a plan for yourself, no matter what position you are in. Don't rely on riding the wave where it takes you. You can either be proactive or reactive to situations like the blizzard or a district's budget.

You may have to go above and beyond to find an answer for how to deal with tough times. Stepping out of your scope of responsibilities and comfort zone is what makes great people great! Don't let a situation take advantage of you, make your mark and seize opportunities that take shape when problems you are confronted with arise.

# *Week 9*

*"Action may not always be happiness, but there is no happiness without action."*

-Benjamin Disraeli

I know we have all heard the saying, "put your money where your mouth is," but what about putting your effort where your mouth is. It is so important to follow through on thoughts or proposed ideas because putting forth that effort may result in great achievements. Following through on ideas with a purpose allows others to see that you are not just all talk. I get so tired of people proposing ideas in meetings, but once they leave the room nobody holds them accountable for their lack of action. Putting forth the effort for the smallest of tasks goes a long way when it involves doing something for another person.

So many people promise others the world, but when it comes to putting their neck, time or effort on the line it seems to fall by the wayside. Make sure you are aware of your thoughts and take the time to follow through.

There are many thoughts you will never actually "see" because you are always thinking and not doing. Thinking or speaking about what you will do does not make you different from others. People are defined by their actions. Don't recommend that something needs to be done, with hopes that OTHERS will make it a reality. Contribution goes a long way, don't make excuses, excuses never make things easier. We should all crave the reputation of being a leader by example. Talk is cheap because you don't have to pay with effort, mistakes, teamwork, time, discipline or consistency.

# Week 10

> "The person who stands out in the crowd demonstrates that he has his own set of values and has a strong sense of self-worth. While the winds of conflicting ideas blow some people away, and the tides of various fads wash others away, he will stand firm."
>
> -David J. Mahoney

To be consistent with your decisions on a daily basis takes extreme focus. After some time it is always easier to just say yes to somebody since it may avoid a minor conflict or make you popular. The problem with always saying yes and keeping others happy means that you are adapting to hundreds of personalities and not being a leader. It is easy to say yes to others just like it is easy NOT to be a leader. By adhering to a rational set of values and beliefs, your decisions will allow you to rest your head on the pillow at night with ease.

As a leader (which is what WE all are in our schools) you must sometimes think with your heart and sometimes with your head. Do not let emotions obstruct your train of thought when making decisions. When dealing with students, colleagues and your family you may tend to go with your heart. The problem is that sometimes, for the good of the group, you must use your head. It is impossible to satisfy everyone and it is okay to make mistakes when making decisions as long as you are not reacting to emotions or other people's pressures.

School budget situations bring to light the heart vs. head decision-making mentality. Of course everyone wants to keep everything but if that's not possible, choices need to be made. Not all choices will be popular but at least we can show respect for the ideas of others. Treating people with respect doesn't mean giving them what they want, but there needs to be a justified reason for the decision being made.

If someone has a problem with a decision you have made it might be their ego talking. You can learn a lot about someone's character after they hear the word "NO." Most times their negative reaction to being criticized or not getting what they want will only verify that the correct decision was made. Being assertive in a humble way can be very empowering. It's not the loudest person or the person with the most to say who makes a great leader. Great leaders are those who offer solutions when asked, don't boast about what they know and don't care who gets the credit.

# *Week 11*

I was introduced to the quote below from Calvin Coolidge while taking a course in college. The lesson I took from it has remained with me ever since. It applies to everyone, in all stages of life, and is a reminder that there are no shortcuts to success. Remember that without honest effort and grit, success is sporadic.

PERSISTENCE

"Nothing in the world can take the place of Persistence.

Talent will not; nothing is more common than unsuccessful men with talent.

Genius will not; unrewarded genius is almost a proverb.

Education will not; the world is full of educated derelicts.

Persistence and determination alone are omnipotent. The slogan 'Press On' has solved and always will solve the problems of the human race."

In a recent study led by Angela Duckworth (a psychologist at the University of Pennsylvania), psychologists performed a study using 190 participants in the Scripps National Spelling Bee. They knew that there were no natural born spellers so they wanted to find out what separated the high level spellers from the average spellers. Their main finding was that deliberate practice consistently helped those who went far in the competition. This may sound very elementary, but the most important "talent" each child possessed was the talent for working hard, even when practicing wasn't fun. Grit and self-control allow people to focus and become talented in a specific area. Self-discipline is a major factor that determines someone's success. Maybe if our students understand that talented/ smart people NEED to work hard, they will see a smaller gap between where they are and where they could be!

# Week 12

> *"Some people think it's holding on that makes one strong. Sometimes it's letting go."*
>
> -Sylvia Robinson

Sometimes we hold on to too much and in the end we are better off mentally and physically by letting go of what we may be emotionally attached to. Emotions are a funny thing. In leadership positions it is so important to not let your emotions guide decision making. Taking emotions out of the equation lets you remain consistent in your decisions and allows you to see things from different perspectives. One quality that many of us possess, but is sometimes used to our disadvantage, is loyalty. When I think of loyalty, only positive vibes come to mind, along with the words trustworthy and honesty. But, sometimes when emotions clog our minds, the loyalty that we all WANT to have can guide us in a negative direction.

Loyalty can be a great trait, but we need to know if we are being loyal to a person or cause that is right and just. Remember that just because you are being "loyal" doesn't mean you are honorable. Always take a step back, take emotion out of the equation, remove the relationship factor and see things through an objective lens. Sometimes we are loyal to a fault and get caught up in something we wouldn't normally be involved with. Supporting your friends, co-workers and family is a great quality, but make sure the support being provided is directed towards the best decision for the group, a good cause and is based on fact, not feelings and emotions.

Being loyal can be an easy way out when you are afraid to tell someone close to you that they may be wrong. The most important type of loyalty is that which is based on good moral principles. Maybe being loyal means that you owe it to a person to make them aware of their negative actions. True loyalty means you have the best interests of someone in mind. Looking out for their best interests may require a reality check when all is said and done. So LET GO of your emotional attachment when being loyal, this will make you and those around you better off in the long run.

# Week 13

"*A pat on the back, though only a few vertebrae removed from a kick in the pants, is miles ahead in results.*"

-Bennett Cerf

As you progress through the school year you are able to identify those students in your class who do not respond well to authority. Authority can be a blessing or a curse. Most times, as figures of authority in a school building, we view ourselves as the "keeper of the law" and the enforcer of the rules. By correcting bad behavior we are only bringing negative attention to a student's actions. What would happen if we acknowledged and recognized the students who are doing something right!?

Whether the "right" thing is expected or extraordinary it will bring a sense of purpose to the student it is directed towards. This can be done in the classroom, hallways or cafeteria and you will see that the student will be overcome with a sense of shock. Even though they may be just acting like themselves, some kids don't know they are doing well because it's in their personality to do so unconsciously. So don't spend time trying to find things that students do wrong, take the time to find them doing something right. We take good behavior for granted because we expect it. Recognize students for doing the right thing no matter how small it may be. This will go a long way toward showing them that we appreciate them doing the expected things. Highlight the positive, people respond better to compliments.

Try complimenting your wife, husband, children or significant other on something that they do every day that is expected of them and not recognized often. They may freeze for a moment and think you are joking!

# Week 14

"*The body of every organization is structured from four kinds of bones. There are the wishbones, who spend all their time wishing someone would do the work. Then there are the jawbones, who do all the talking, but little else. The knucklebones knock everything anybody else tries to do. Fortunately, in every organization there are also the backbones, who get under the load and do most of the work.*"

-Leo Aikman

I think at some point in our lives we need to find out what drives us. Do you wake up in the morning dreading work or are you thankful for another day that allows you to come to your school? Obviously family should be the most important thing in our lives and to most people that is a no-brainer. How we perform in the workplace should be important to all of us as well and we need to find out what makes each one of us tick.

For many people, there needs to be an incentive involved for them to perform at a high level. Incentives can include monetary benefits and awards, but to some the incentive is intangible. Selfless people make less work for others. What I mean by that is, if you consider others in your decisions or the ripple effects of your effort (or lack of effort), the incentive is wanting to make those around you better off.

What's the incentive to call parents if their child's grade is dipping, to teach your rear-end off, to go above and beyond your scope of responsibility, to come to work when you're tired, to get creative with lessons, to motivate students, etc.....

That incentive SHOULD BE to make everyone better around you! Don't put colleagues or students in a "bad spot." Ask yourself each day, "Did I do all I could for this student?" or "Did I do all I could for my school?"

I saw a great sign the other day that said....TEACHING: IN IT FOR THE OUTCOME, NOT THE INCOME

Do great things without expecting recognition, the reward will come to you when you least expect it…

# Week 15

Advice for high school graduates:

Top Ten List

1. Never overreact, don't let emotions get the best of you

2. Be selfless

3. Listen to others when conversing don't just think about what YOU will say next

4. Do not judge others

5. Stand tall and be consistent with your beliefs/decisions

6. Accept what is happening around you, you can only control YOUR reactions to external factors

7. Welcome change, it will help you grow

8. Be able to think with your heart AND head when a decision is difficult

9. Say Thank You and acknowledge others who help you

10. Leave your ego, impatience and complaining at the door to guarantee a great day

That's my $0.02…

# Week 16

*"The ultimate measure of a man is not where he stands in moments of comfort and convenience, but where he stands at times of challenge and controversy."*
-Martin Luther King, Jr.

We learn a lot about people when their backs are "against the wall" or when they are given options to choose from. For fear of being exposed, many people will hide from controversy or not stand up for what they believe in. It is easy to follow the pack and fly under the radar, but sometimes we are forced to make a decision when one will not be made for us. When you are not used to being trusted or believed in, the fear of Free Will lingers. Free Will allows you to follow your gut instinct and forces you to be held accountable for your decisions. Free Will sounds like a liberating term but for many it can be debilitating when they are not used to being held accountable for their actions or choices. To be a leader they say you must separate yourself from the crowd but that separation or freedom from the majority sometimes leaves you on an island surrounded by a very reflective body of water.

When making decisions for yourself, your students or your family it is important to be consistent and fair. When you are on your "island" you will have nobody to blame but yourself for your actions/decisions and for some people this can be daunting. We are all leaders amongst leaders and at times we will not be able to make the popular decision. Don't fear what others think of you because when you take a look at yourself in your island's reflective water, you should be proud of what you represent.

# Week 17

Trust is one of the most sacred things in our lives. You cannot purchase it, it is earned over long periods of time and once it is tainted, it might as well not exist. To have trust is to be secure with those you deal with at work and your personal life. Sometimes it can be taken for granted when it is not tested. Trust is never tested more than in times of turmoil and adversity. Sure, at times we will all have to be brutally honest with one another, but at the end of the day it doesn't matter who is right. As long as the job gets done according to our standard of performance and choices are made for the right reasons, we can understand that we are all one piece of a large puzzle.

Nothing upsets a school leader more than to have external factors alter the way they do business in a school. It is almost like a parent telling a coach who to play in a game, without knowing the chemistry of the team or how it will impact the team's psyche. When outside circumstances affect your home (in this case your school) you immediately get defensive. We can only control our reactions to certain things and we will only find solace when we realize that most things happen for a reason. At school we have a reason for treating people with respect (when deserved) and our approach to business can't change no matter how erratic the external factors are. Remember that as professionals we have a responsibility to be the best we can be. Sometimes doing a little extra separates you from the pack and improves your school community as a whole. Will your legacy be one of *did what I had to do* OR *did what I could for all?*

# *Week 18*

Seeing things from your usual perspective may not allow you to see what is really going on. Your perspective is something that has grown inside of you and is based on your environment growing up and life/work experiences. A perspective therefore will usually include emotions that are attached to the experiences you have had. Thinking a certain way about things will tend to become a habit for some people and cloud their reality since they may only know THEIR way.

I literally had to change my perspective on things when I was fitted for my first pair of eyeglasses. I only knew one way of viewing the world and never gave a second thought to how cloudy my vision actually was. My eye doctor had been telling me for over 15 years that I should get glasses for reading and computer use but I always thought I survived fine without them. Anyway, when I first put them on I thought something was wrong with the prescription since everything looked strange through the lenses. Turns out everything was correct and I just needed to get used to the new lens through which I would be viewing things.

Please consider walking into your school building through a different entrance each morning, stand in a different location in the classroom or put yourself in a student's shoes every now and then. Your perspective on certain things may seem just fine, but are you really taking the time to change things up to see "what could have been." Habits and routine are easily formed but sometimes we need to stray from the path and take advantage of detours. We may be missing out on things in life when we focus on getting from point A to B. Stubbornness or comfort levels may have us refusing to really see (C) what is going on!

# Week 19

"*The only way to make a man trustworthy is to trust him.*"

-Henry Lewis Stimson

I know that I mentioned the value of trust in a prior message but I'd like to touch upon how we can develop it naturally. Project Adventure classes facilitate "trust falls" which require people falling to trust that others will catch them, given they have zero chance of catching themselves. This is an exercise that is as challenging to the mind as it can be to the body. Many people who have a hard time trusting tend to not like to feel vulnerable. Feeling vulnerable requires you to open a small window that may let in failure, hurt or mistakes.

Trusting in systems and processes is hard for most because usually the result or solution takes time. In our digital age where information and answers are provided at the speed of light, I feel that our society expects the development of things to occur quicker than they should. By rushing to do something we are not allowing development, whether it be through thought or action, to take place. Expecting instant gratification is our society's downfall which is why conflict occurs due to a breakdown or "lull" in communication.

I find myself feeling the pressure of not allowing a mistake as my 2-year-old daughter experiments with EVERYTHING. The more independent she seems to become, the more I fear for her hurting herself as she must learn from mistakes (sometimes resulting in Band-Aids, both figuratively and literally). I find that I have my hand out to prevent her from falling when I'm around her, but if I don't let her fall she may never learn how to pick herself up or prevent it from happening again. So in essence I am creating a false reality that may not allow her to "learn" through a developmental process.

It was brought to my attention by my wife that nature doesn't rush things, yet everything seems to be accomplished in the end. If we can understand the necessity of letting things naturally occur in the classroom and in the flow of our personal lives, we will overcome impatience and lack of trust in the future.

# Week 20

E very morning that you wake up, you have a choice…..

To bring a positive attitude to your day

To try to make things work when they don't seem to be working

To put ego aside for the greater whole

To not over-analyze situations

To understand that you cannot change people but only your reaction to them

To attract others to work with you & not have them doubt themselves

To keep in mind that any angst or complaining is only taking time away from being happy

To be happy rather than right

Remember that when our "time is up" there will not be a score on the headstone saying you won or lost, but that you are missed because you made others happier...

# Week 21

## VULNERABILITY

As professionals we are always told to follow a certain code of conduct and understand building/district policies. What they don't tell our new teachers during their orientation is that rules alone will not allow you to make a connection with students. Sometimes we need to let our guard down in order to build up relationships. By sharing a personal story that may help you relate to a troubled student or just by speaking from your heart, colleagues and students will value the genuineness. For some, sharing times of personal weakness or trouble can make them feel vulnerable. Feeling vulnerable is an unwanted feeling for most, but if you allow it to occur, trusting relationships will develop like never before!

We had a recent incident with a 9th grade student who was afraid to enter the building and once he did he sprawled out on the hallway floor refusing to go to class. As he lay there silent and staring in the distance I had a one-on-one moment with him that allowed me to share some fears of my own. "Breaking it down" for the student allowed me to build him up. By talking to him as a trusting individual and not an authority figure I was able to break down those walls that many students form in their minds.

Because of our society today, people feel the need to lie or cover things up for fear of being judged. If fear of being judged inhibits your ability to be genuine, please know that those who do the judging usually have the biggest fears/insecurities of all, otherwise they wouldn't care about other people's business.

# Week 22

## SCARS

*"It's the people without the scars, those are the people you have to worry about."*

-Eddie Vedder

Sometimes you have to get "kicked to the curb" in order to develop a sense of grit inside that makes you resilient to any circumstances that are thrust upon you. This grit can make you stronger, giving you a sense of confidence that can't be bought…since you know that you've survived the toughest of times. It is the people who have never had to experience strife, loss or failure who may not know what they are truly made of since they never had to overcome something out of their control. To have scars means that you are battle tested, have been knocked down before and experienced mistakes. Those who have been forced to experience "lows" understand what it takes to rise up. These people tend to be hungrier for the prize or willing to sacrifice more than those who have never been forced to sacrifice anything.

When building a team of individuals to achieve a common goal it would be wise to include people who have achieved something from the ground up, value trust and people who don't need a PR firm to prove how valuable they are. Just like a cut on the skin can only heal from the inside going outward, true persevering can only happen if you possess a foundation that cannot be cracked by pressure. From the core of your being, a solid foundation is needed in order to improve yourself. Within that foundation lie the advice and good qualities you took from those who might have been lost along the journey of your life.

Keep in mind that while most people fear the act of suffering, you may not appreciate the highs as much as you should unless you've experienced the lows.

# Week 23

"We're brought up, unfortunately, to think that nobody should make mistakes. Most children get de-geniused by the love and fear of their parents-- that they might make a mistake. But all my advances were made by mistakes. You uncover what IS when you get rid of what ISN'T."

- Buckminster Fuller

The lens through which we view life must be clear. Many students make mistakes, behaviorally or academically. These mistakes are not the result of someone being a bad person, but a good person making a poor decision. As long as we teach our students to learn from mistakes, they will begin to focus on seeing success without worrying about failure. Fact is, life is about experiences, it is important to learn lessons from each one and be conscious (figuratively speaking!) when they occur. Being aware is vital so you do not miss opportunities for enjoyment and reflection. Too many people (especially students) live life unconsciously, never acknowledging the fact that they have certain flaws and they are afraid to admit their faults. What many people don't remember is that once you are aware of your faults, it then becomes possible to work on improving yourself, which will make you a better person. By denying what you really are, you are only denying yourself a rich, fruitful life.

# Week 24

Here is a little change of pace…this just shows that open and honest communication, though sometimes frowned upon by others, is the best policy! Remember to be yourself, don't be ashamed of who you are and be proud of what you represent. The applicant below didn't allow his identity to be lost in the formalities of society. Do not allow procedures and cultural norms to prevent YOU from being YOU while working at your respective school! Hard work, honesty and grit can take you far in life…please read below:

Judging by the response that has greeted a particularly candid cover letter, you might get the sense that Wall Street executives spend 90 percent of their days being lied to. An undergraduate applicant for a summer internship at an investment bank described himself as having "no unbelievably special skills or genius eccentricities" in a cover letter to one of the firm's execs. The exec then forwarded the letter around Wall Street, saying, "this might be the best cover letter I've ever received."

### Here's the full letter:

My name is (BLOCKED) and I am an undergraduate finance student at (BLOCKED). I met you the summer before last at Smith & Wollensky's in New York when I was touring the east coast with my uncle, (BLOCKED). I just wanted to thank you for taking the time to talk with me that night.

I am writing to inquire about a possible summer internship in your office. I am aware it is highly unusual for undergraduates from average universities like (BLOCKED) to intern at (BLOCKED), but nevertheless I was hoping you might make an exception. I am extremely interested in investment banking and would love nothing more than to learn under your tutelage. I have no qualms about fetching coffee, shining shoes or picking up laundry, and will work for next to nothing. In all honesty, I just want to be around professionals in the industry and gain as much knowledge as I can.

I won't waste your time inflating my credentials, throwing around exaggerated job titles, or feeding you a line of crap about how my past experiences and skill set align perfectly for an investment banking internship. The truth is I have no unbelievably special skills or genius eccentricities, but I do have a near perfect GPA and will work hard for you. I've interned for Merrill Lynch in the Wealth Management Division and taken an investment banking class at (BLOCKED), for whatever that is worth.

I am currently awaiting admission results for (BLOCKED) Masters of Science in Accountancy program, which I would begin this fall if admitted. I am also planning on attending law school after my master's program, which we spoke about in New York. I apologize for the blunt nature of my letter, but I hope you seriously consider taking me under your wing this summer. I have attached my resume for your review. Feel free to call me at (BLOCKED) or email at (BLOCKED). Thank you for your time.

# Week 25

*"Where there is a void, negativity will fill it."*

-Jon Gordon

M any students may not identify themselves as being "part" of their school culture. A lack of connection to school usually means that a student will deviate from what the school is trying to accomplish. They won't have a vested interest in the bigger picture and where they fit in. How many times do we try to get students involved in some aspect of school life, such as clubs, music or athletics? Fact is, LIFE IS ABOUT CONNECTIONS. Without a connection to something or somebody you are on an island. When we are young we try hard to be part of a group and that connection gives us confidence. As we get older we naturally tend to break off connections with those who are weaker than others.

When a connection or bond does not exist a void opens up. Some of us may not know a void exists in our lives, but if we take a step back, we may find ourselves overcompensating in other areas to fill it. Some students do not have the ability to fill their void in a positive manner. They will find themselves taking part in unproductive, negative activities as they float on through a school day.

So I humbly ask everyone to help students find a connection in your building. The stronger their connection to school, the stronger their connection will be to your class and their studies. Strong bonds with solid foundations culminate in long lasting relationships and positive results. Making a connection with students can happen if they see you at one of their games, a concert or simply asking them about their weekend. The connections made outside the classroom may pay huge dividends when it comes to lesson implementation and student performance. Students want to work hard for people they trust and feel connected to.

# Week 26

Our lives are based on relationships. The better they are, the more we enjoy life. Relationships are something you cannot buy. It takes effort by both sides to make them work, but the more you give, the more rewarding they are. Unfortunately miscommunication and assumptions are the cause of many problems in relationships. If you don't hear something from the "horse's mouth," take it as untrue. Too many negative emotions are wasted on thinking about what others say. There are few people who we can really trust with our personal information in life. Unfortunately it takes time to find out who those people are and it may hurt when you find out who you can't trust.

Each day brings many tests of your beliefs, morals and values. Instead of thinking poorly about others, focus your energy on the people who care about and support you through thick and thin....the score if people are keeping one, will take care of itself. Let's be thankful for the positive family, work and personal relationships we have. If there is someone you would like to reach out to whether it be to catch up or clear things up, make it happen, the first step starts with you!

The relationships and people your schools have are what make them a special place. Even though some days can be tough, having one kid say thank you can make it all worth it.

# Week 27

If you think about each day of our lives, we spend approximately 8 hours sleeping (if you have kids this is a bonus), 8 hours working, and the other 8 hours we have for ourselves/other responsibilities. So 1/3 of our day is allocated just for us. Now over a 30-year career in education we will have approximately 1/3 of that time for ourselves, making it 10 years. What we do with our personal time can allow us to go from good to great. Will we spend a majority of time watching TV or on Facebook? Do we try to use personal time to better ourselves mentally and physically? Do we have conversations with friends & loved ones to allow relationships to grow?

Everyone's answer will differ but the key here is to not let your day control you. We all have the same amount of time each day, but why do some feel that there is never enough time to do what they really want to do? By attacking your daily routine you take back your day without letting your day take you. We all need time for ourselves, otherwise our minds never get to focus on our daily goals and we are at the mercy of others and the clock each day.

Schedule time for yourself, otherwise you will try jamming it in at the end of each day when "time is up" or you are too tired to accomplish anything. The 1/3 is something that people may feel is out of their control, but once you strategize a bit, you won't find yourself "hoping" to make the 1/3 worthwhile.

# *Week 28*

Architect Frank Lloyd Wright told how a lecture he received at the age of nine helped set his philosophy of life. An uncle, a stolid, no-nonsense type, had taken him for a long walk across a snow-covered field. At the far side, his uncle told him to look back at their two sets of tracks.

> "See, my boy," he said, "how your footprints go aimlessly back and forth from those trees, to the cattle, back to the fence and then over there where you were throwing sticks? But notice how my path comes straight across, directly to my goal. You should never forget this lesson!"
>
> "And I never did," Wright said, grinning. "I determined right then not to miss most things in life, as my uncle had."

> - John Keasler

It is so important to be flexible in life. We are taught to have systems and processes in an effort to streamline things. We need to enjoy the detours that life brings. Just like during our school day, you may be heading from point A to B with a clear goal in mind, and if you rush by a colleague in the hall you may be missing something. Even in class, a student may have a random question and if you steamroll over it, you could be missing out on a learning opportunity or a chance to develop a closer bond with that student.

I am guilty of taking the direct path many times, and I would love to speak with everyone I encounter, but it's just not possible given the craziness of a school day. The "got a minutes" may delay my course of action a bit, but sometimes they bring a pleasant surprise that I was not expecting. We need to keep the "minutes" in mind because they seem to get lost in our rapidly passing life.

# Week 29

*"If you're not learning while you're earning, you're cheating yourself out of the better portion of your compensation."*

-Napoleon Hill

The pursuit of knowledge should be a priority, for our work related tasks and overall well-being. We should encourage our students to become life-long learners and we should be the same. It's always nice to hear about the positive conversations that occur during staff development periods that take place throughout the year.

Many of you are excited to share your best practices with others in your schools. Please remember that the only way to achieve your goals is to take that initial step. Whether you make a mistake or forget to include something, you are still making progress because conversations are taking place and ideas are being put on paper. Things may not be perfect the first time through, but the fact that you are working together allows you to put forth a well-rounded product that represents all the great ideas and minds from each classroom.

Sometimes we question the reason why we are doing something before we begin the journey, but as we get in the "thick of it," the vision and purpose become more visible. Just know that when the finished product presents itself before you, you may realize that you learned a lot about yourself and teammates through the process. Sometimes people rush to get to the end of a journey, but it's important (as crazy as it sounds) to enjoy the rough road along the way. Along that road are the stories and battles that make our bonds stronger in the long run. Remember that a true colleague walks in when others walk out!

# Week 30

*"What do we live for if not to make the world less difficult for each other?"*

-George Eliot

I wonder about this on a daily basis as we move through our hectic days. It seems that many people are more concerned with being right rather than just being happy. The amount of energy people spend trying to prove themselves right must be exhausting. In the scheme of life it is important to understand that always being right doesn't always make you, or others around you, happy. The most unhappy people spend too much time proving they are right. Whether it's complaining or not conceding a belief because you want to validate your position, these "ego trippers" will suck the life out of you! We all need to understand that feeling a sense of worth shouldn't correlate to the amount of times you are right, if anything your worth should be measured by how well you work within a team (family) concept and make rational decisions.

It's interesting how many people attempt to validate their position/rank by making decisions harder than they have to be. By complicating matters, you may be making people's lives more difficult while not making a difference. People will respect you more if you open yourself up to some criticism and allow other ideas to enter your sphere of thinking. By taking chances and trying to create solutions rather than critiquing the ideas that exist, you will find happiness. So remember that each day you go to work you should empower others you work with by listening to their ideas and if their ideas happen to be "right" just let it be and learn to accept it. I once heard a saying, "that which you resist, will persist." When you resist change or other people's ideas, the frustration that occurs will remain until you loosen up the reins and stop trying to control.

# *Week 31*

*"We are always complaining that our days are few,
and acting as though there would be no end to them."*

-Seneca

Why is it that we consider people with complex ideas as smart or sometimes brilliant? There is a difference between being smart and being unnecessarily complex. We only have so much time to take care of things while at work and at home. Why do we make things more complex than they have to be? I feel that some people create challenges in their lives for no reason. Challenge yourself for purposeful things in life, not tasks that can be solved simply. It's okay to make things simple at work and at home, doing so doesn't mean you are not intelligent. People try to make themselves seem more intelligent by "blowing up" minor issues and using EDUbabble (the art of using educational buzz words to make simple ideas more complex) to make things seem more complex than they really are.

The smart way of conducting business is to make policies and processes less complex. Less complexity means that people will think less and act more. If I needed to evaluate someone's intellectual prowess, I would consider the person who turns a complex process into a simple one, the smarter person. Smart is not a person who spends time complicating matters to remain in control or to make their job seem more important than it really is. Developing ideas for an organization is not about rank and position; it is about doing what is best for those who carry out those policies on a daily basis. As long as the guidelines are sound the purpose is only driven by WANT TO rather than HAVE TO.

Hopefully we all take this into account as we enforce guidelines in our classrooms, offices and personal lives. So remember, life is too short to waste energy and race against the clock. The number of days we have need to be spent with good intentions since we will only be known for how we affected others, not how we took care of ourselves...

# Week 32

## SIMPLICITY

To most it means easy, to others it means classy, to some maybe dumbing something down. The beauty of keeping things simple is that lines are never blurred and the natural form of something is preserved in its truest state. Acoustic music is broken down into simplistic parts allowing the listener to hear the passion behind the song, the best restaurants in the world keep things simple by focusing on making fewer meals more perfect and becoming less distracted with technological gadgets at home allows a family to spend time on strengthening bonds. To me, simplicity in life seems to allow people to zoom in on what's at stake or what's important.

Simplifying things at work and in our personal lives makes everything more efficient. Sometimes we complicate things in the workplace for fear of that rare instance when a random event may occur. The what-ifs will take care of themselves if the procedures, relationships and rules are more about quality than quantity. Between TV, DVDs, iPods, iPads and video games some people can alleviate problems by allowing these complicated distractions to consume them. Alleviating stress or an ongoing problem does not mean the issue goes away. Sometimes the over-complication of our lives leads to problems that shouldn't exist in the first place. While most people in our society feel that "more" is the answer, they need to realize that simplicity is the true key to happiness.

# Week 33

Recalling the pep talk he gave the Dallas Cowboys before their victory in the 1993 Super Bowl game:

> "I told them that if I laid a two-by-four across the room everybody there could walk across it and not fall, because our focus would be that we were going to walk that two-by-four. But if I put that same two-by-four ten stories high between two buildings, only a few would make it, because the focus would be on falling."
> -Jimmy Johnson

Sometimes the reason people don't persevere is because the lenses through which they view life are focused on failing, not succeeding. To be a leader you must always make the most out of the hand you are dealt and expect to overcome challenges. You can't always ask for a new set of cards since that would allow everyone to succeed. By choosing to work or "play" under the perfect circumstances means that adjustments and challenges are not welcomed. As leaders we have to get the most out of ourselves and empower those around us.

Problem solving occurs when you understand that a set of circumstances will not be changing on its own. By complaining and saying that things aren't in your favor, you are no different than anyone else who has not succeeded. ANYONE can succeed when all the pieces line up or when you are dealt "4 Aces" in your hand. Anybody can hit a pitch that is thrown over the plate, at the right speed. The best and most memorable hitters are those that can crush pitches out of the zone…that's what creates a legacy!

So what will your legacy be? Will you be remembered as someone who sought out adjustments to alter bad situations or will you be known as someone who can only succeed when the going is good. Remember to savor any challenges that come before you. See them as opportunities that may open other doors. Know that by overcoming them you will be stronger and learn more about yourself in the end. Also, remind students to approach exams with a positive mindset. Many of them default to believing they didn't study enough right before they take a test, essentially focusing on falling (like Jimmy's quote). When they encounter the one question they don't know their self-fulfilling prophecy is realized and their confidence begins to dwindle. A strong mindset will keep them and all of us focused on our goal, even if the cards are stacked against us.

# Week 34

*"I wept because I had no shoes, until I saw a man who had no feet."*

-Ancient Persian Saying

Why is it that we don't appreciate things until they are gone? When you lose something or somebody you love and cherish, you learn very quickly to appreciate what you had previously. How great life would be if we woke up each day and acknowledged what we have before our day begins. Having this conversation with yourself may be the most worthwhile one you have all day. Next time you feel stressed, think of all the things/people that you are thankful for in your life. It is impossible to be stressed and grateful at the same time. Don't realize what you HAD after it is taken away. Recognize what you HAVE so that your energy will be focused on the important things in life.

It's funny how we approach each workday as a routine and something ordinary. What we need to do is be thankful for our health, the fact that we can see & hear, our friends, family, being able to walk, and our home. So next time you have car trouble, be thankful you have enough money to own a car. The next time you feel that you didn't get enough sleep, be thankful that you were able to sleep under a roof. For some people being able to do/have these things would make their day extraordinary, so why isn't each day extraordinary to us?

# Week 35

*"Everyone should have a sense of urgency – it is getting a lot done in a short period of time in a calm confident manner."*

-Bob Proctor

There is a huge difference between people who have a sense of urgency and those who do not. When you need to get something done for yourself or for your colleagues, ask yourself if you are being as proactive as you can be. The common denominator in all of your life's issues is YOU. If things continually seem to be problematic, you need to stop blaming others and look at how you can change your approach to situations.

Having urgency doesn't mean you need to show panic or that you need to run around being busy. Urgency is a focus and desire to get something done to the best of your ability. Just because somebody is exhibiting a calm demeanor doesn't dismiss the fact that they may be stressed. As educators, leaders and parents we should always remain calm, be strong and know that whatever stress or franticness we are exuding will become contagious. Sometimes we need to ask…why do I always experience stress with this or why do I always have a problem with that?

# Week 36

During a school year you will deal with personal and work related challenges. You will experience triumph and failure as well as surprises and disappointments. Every school year helps us learn the lesson of "you can only control YOUR reaction to external forces."

I wish I could say it will only get easier, but the journey wouldn't be as exciting if everything was easy. The only thing that will allow you to overcome challenges is an attitude consisting of GRIT. The intrinsic value of being a professional is important since we do not receive bonuses or monetary incentives to overcome obstacles as educators.

Please remember these words as you move forward in your career:

The 6 most important words are:

"I admit I made a mistake."

The 5 most important words are:

"I am proud of you."

The 4 most important words are:

"What is your opinion?"

The 3 most important words are:

"If you please."

The 2 most important words are:

"Thank you."

The 1 most important word is:

"We"

# Week 37

*"What you are afraid to do is a clear indicator of the next thing you need to do."*

-Unknown

This should be the theme every year in our classrooms so that we may grow and learn more about ourselves. Let's step out of comfort zones and bust through anticipation walls. When we think or anticipate too much we tend to freeze up and not allow something to take place when it was intended to. Avoidance sometimes means that we are afraid to find out if we are weak in a particular area. Let US and our STUDENTS put egos aside and trust in the environment in which we/they are a part of.

# Week 38

*"Some can't distinguish between being busy and being productive. They are human windmills, flailing at work, but actually accomplishing little."*

-Caroline Donnelly

Take into account how many tasks you are responsible for each day, at home and at work. It is important to focus your energy in order to maximize your time doing things that you love. For everyone, the things we love differ from person to person, but remember to not allow the little things to distract you from what you value in life. If your busy tendencies take time away from what you "want" to be doing, you need to re-evaluate your approach to things that may "seem" important. Work smarter not harder!!

# Week 39

"*People are always blaming their circumstances for what they are. I do not believe in circumstances. The people who get on in this world are the people who get up and look for the circumstances they want, and if they cannot find them, make them.*"

-George Bernard Shaw

It is so important to walk into work with a positive attitude. If you feel defeated before the day begins, your self-fulfilling prophecy will take shape as the day progresses. As a leader, both in the building and classroom, colleagues/students will approach you with problems and negativity throughout the day (acting like human dump trucks). The higher you start on the "it's going to be okay scale" the better your day will go. It is very difficult to allow these energy drainers to pass you by and not care about their problems when in essence you need them to build a good culture in the building and in your classroom. If you are genuine and want to help people this will drag you into their world for a brief moment, but when that moment expires you need to let the garbage truck move on to the next house and not take-on their issues as your own. Doing so will allow you to focus on your daily goals and appreciate the good things you have going for you.

Recommended Book: *The Law of the Garbage Truck* by David Pollay

# Week 40

*"An ego trip is something that never gets you anywhere."*

-Suzan L. Wiener

Pay attention to how many people use "I" and "My" more than "We" and "Us" during your day. This self-centered way of thinking inhibits so much progress in our daily interactions. When people are focused on themselves, the conversation never goes anywhere because they bring every story back to THEM. Usually those who focus on themselves tend to miss out on learning opportunities because they think their way is always right and they always have a story to top yours.

When speaking with other principals I try to catch how many times they use "I" and "My" when talking about custodians, security guards, clerical or staff. I could never say "my custodians"…"my school" or "my staff" because we are all part of the same team. Our main interest should be to give our students the best experience possible (and it's okay if we have fun while doing it).

Competition in life is natural, but challenge yourself, don't compete against someone else's accomplishments. Let your actions speak for you and people will respect you more for it. We are defined by our daily actions, not our words. Bragging and boasting only amplifies the ego, so please remember to leave your ego at the door each day you go to school and as a team you will accomplish more.

# Week 41

During a hurricane in the Northeast region in October 2012 there was a lot of time to think with our electricity being down for 7 days. When I started to think of words to describe what we all felt or went through the "S" and the "A" came to mind first and it started a chain reaction....the name of the hurricane was SANDY and she was not as sweet as the one from the movie Grease!

Sacrifice - We had no choice but to sacrifice. Sacrifices included time, comfort, routines, belongings, peace of mind. The more we sacrifice the more likely we will value what we have. Many people sacrificed things for loved ones and friends because IN A TIME OF NEED THERE IS NO ROOM FOR GREED. The smaller our world becomes the less likely we will understand the bigger picture. Life is about what you do for others, not what you do for yourself. Giving our time to help people, whether donating items or lending a helping hand makes a huge difference.

Appreciation - Time to re-evaluate the needs and wants in our lives. After seeing the people who needed to use the Red Cross shelter in our building, it inspired me to volunteer some time outside of school to help those who are less fortunate. It is important to stay grounded and not gloat or brag about the things we have. People will never look at gas stations or cars the same as they did prior to the hurricane. Besides food, clothing and shelter, family time was something that was valued during that week. Due to the lack of electricity and television people began focusing on the people under their roof rather than American Idol or Dancing with the Stars!

New Relationships - A common enemy or situation makes it easy to form bonds with others. In this case the enemy was discomfort, fear and helplessness. It seemed that many people felt helpless and with everyone being in the same boat, people were more understanding. The effects of Hurricane Sandy had families talking again, people knocking on a neighbor's door for the first time in years to see if they were alright and parents spending quality time with their children as opposed to playing a DVD for them.

Decision-making - Costs vs. Benefits in life...to drive or not to drive, that's the question! Do I or don't I prepare? I think we all learned that you can never over-prepare. We can make choices but must decide if the calculated risk is worth the benefit. We all made decisions prior to the hurricane. Are we happy with the ones we made? What would we change for next time?

<u>Youth</u> - We have to appreciate the optimism and fearlessness of young people. As the storm was in full force I watched my daughter still want to play and loved the fact that her parents were by her side. What she did was enjoy the moment. Kids take fear out of the equation when you observe them during difficult times since they don't dwell on things. A child's "no fear" mentality and love for the present moment is something that adults lose as they get older. Less thinking and anticipation actually eliminates fear, sometimes we over-think which actually hinders our ability to be in the moment. As you go forward, let's all live our lives like children but not act childish!

# Week 42

"We all have something to give. So if you know how to read, find someone who can't. If you've got a hammer find a nail. If you're not hungry, not lonely, not in trouble---seek out someone who is."

-George H. W. Bush

As you begin each day in school remember that there are many young people who are looking for guidance and structure (whether they know it or not). Some students are self-sufficient while others may need a nudge during the year. Some need to be pushed to work harder in class or some may need to be told to do their homework. Outside of the schoolwork aspect of a day are kids who need a nudge in a positive direction. These are the kids in the halls who walk along the wall or the kids in the cafeteria who sit alone (maybe not wanting to).

As I walked through one of the cafeterias during my first year as a high school principal I noticed a female student sitting alone with her head down, doing some homework. All I needed to do was say "hi" and her face lit up. You could tell she was just wanting to talk to somebody. A two-minute conversation allowed me to learn many things about her, so that when I saw her again, we would have some common ground.

Relationships are built one at a time. If you put the time into them, there's no telling how strong they can become. All I ask is that WE ALL take the time to build and foster positive relationships in our schools. Having good relationships between all who work/learn has more of an effect than any policy or code of conduct we can produce. The many rules and demands we place on our students will only work if the "human" side of us implements them correctly. Let's face it, we are in the people business and solid, meaningful relationships drive our day. Be conscious of your interactions with others and make them worthwhile and purposeful.

# Week 43

*"Whoever you are, there is some younger person who thinks you are perfect. There is some work that will never be done if you don't do it. There is someone who would miss you if you were gone. There is a place that you alone can fill."*

-Jacob M. Braude

Obtaining material objects does not define who we are as individuals. It is not the size of the house that matters, it's the memories that are made while living in it. As educators we have the greatest job in the world because we have a group of young men and women who we can positively influence on a daily basis. The service and effort we put into our students will eventually be the memories they take with them. Next time you are teaching a lesson remember that you have the power to inspire. The information that you pass on whether it be curriculum related or a life lesson will be utilized by some of your students. It is this type of service that makes you an important piece of each student's puzzle. Some students' puzzles have many missing pieces and some only need a few. Fact is, we are old enough to have learned from our mistakes which makes our lessons even more valuable to the young people in your building.

The individual "service" that you provide each day in your respective school should not be lost in the numbers and data of any state guidelines or scores. We tend to get caught up with numbers and rank in life, when we should only be concerned with service, and how we are taking care of our students and loved ones outside of work. Teachers become worried about test scores but if you focus your attention on providing for your students, the score will take care of itself. We all need to learn to stop and breathe once in a while. Resting in peace should not just be a statement used for those who have passed on. Why can't we rest and have inner peace now! Remember why you are here…..to serve your students and your colleagues in the best way possible. Throw egos and the "king of the hill" mentality out the window. I am sure that throughout our careers we will derive much more satisfaction from a student who says thank you than from state test score data. If you want to be first in the eyes of others, you need to put yourself last.

# Week 44

"*Mastering others is strength. Mastering yourself is true power.*"

-Lao Tzu

As most of us progress through the typical 30-year educational career, we will all probably say in the end, "Yes, I am a master of my craft, I know my content inside & out and can handle any class." But as we go through those 30 years are we only teaching each day or learning ourselves? It is important to take advantage of the many interactions we have with students and colleagues. We all have a role in the most interactive, relationship-based job in the world and it is our responsibility to not only help others learn, but to learn more about ourselves in the process. Without reflecting on the many interactions we have in one day, we will never grow professionally or as individuals. So let's not take the approach each day of "let me show everyone what I know." Instead we need to be thankful for what we know and what we can share, but also remember to listen and take in the ideas/actions of others. Based on experience we will be able to master most situations within the school setting. But let's remember that to master ourselves, we need to remain humble and welcome all interactions, no matter how difficult they may be. It is through the most difficult times that we learn the most about ourselves. Remember that self-mastery is the basis for success, for yourself as well as with others.

# Week 45

Sometimes we need to make short term sacrifices for long term gains. It is important to keep your "eye on the prize" but our daily actions will dictate whether or not that goal is achieved. One of the only things you may need to sacrifice in order to achieve great things is comfort. I have never met anybody who achieved something without taking a risk. Too many people are filled with "what ifs" and hearing leaders start most of their sentences with "what my concern is" or "what my fear is"...actually concerns me!

By forcing yourself to be uncomfortable you will learn more about yourself. Refusing to accept the risk sometimes means that we are afraid to uncover or bring attention to weaknesses we may have. The great thing about weaknesses, is that they may eventually be our greatest strength. If we overcome them, then we essentially become a vital cog in helping others overcome those same weaknesses. A sense of purpose will grow as you try to help others through their troubles as well. Attacking a challenge is something we tell our students so let's make sure we practice what we preach, both in our personal and work lives. It is also important to take things day by day.... by looking too far down the road we tend to mentally run out of gas before we even start the trip.

# Week 46

It's Not the Critic Who Counts:

*Not the man who points out how the strong man stumbles or where the doer of deeds could have done better. The credit belongs to the man who is actually in the arena, whose face is marred by dust and sweat and blood, who strives valiantly, who errs and comes up short again and again, because there is no effort without error, but he who knows the great enthusiasms, the great devotions who spends himself for a worthy cause, who at the best knows in the end, the triumph of high achievement and who, at the worst, if he fails, at least he fails while Daring Greatly, so that his place shall never be with those Cold and Timid Souls who new neither Victory nor Defeat.*

-Theodore Roosevelt

As a leader in your classroom or among the students in the halls, it's important to keep your decision-making consistent. Because we work in the public sector, "the public" will be the first to critique something they feel is wrong. Even though critics exist, it is important to think about where the negative words are coming from. Because our beliefs are challenged on a daily basis it is important to not compromise sound judgment when pressure is felt by students or parents. I often tell parents that it's much easier for 30 students to follow one belief system than for a teacher or coach to follow 30 different belief systems within a class/team. We are all leaders in our respective buildings, no matter what our position is. If students follow our good example then that should be satisfaction enough in knowing that what we are doing is right.

*Week 47*

*"You don't get harmony when everybody sings the same note."*

-Doug Floyd

Diversity of talent and thought adds flavor to the workplace, opening the lines of communication and teamwork. It is so important to be honest to yourself and others in your building. People tend to become so worried about procedures, rules and the "chain of command" that they lose their identity. Don't be afraid to make a decision on your own. You were hired as a professional and your professional judgment is valued. Take comfort in knowing that coming up with a solution to a problem rather than presenting a problem to somebody else is appreciated. Be an individual and take pride in the fact that you can handle situations on your own. Most mistakes that occur in a school are fixable and can be learned from. Don't conform to the point that your personality and decision-making skills have trouble shining through. People will respect you more for being who you are, not taking yourself too seriously and sharing your opinions. Remember to be true to yourself and success will find you.

# Week 48

Being true to yourself and who you are is so important in the long term. Eventually lies and avoidance of issues will catch up to you because anything that you resist will persist. Learn to accept flaws and people/events for what they are while being thankful for all that is positive in your life. A friend of mine introduced me to the *Man in the Glass* poem a while back. I had to share it with everyone because we should also be thankful for who we are and for coming out of struggles on top whenever the odds were against us...please substitute woman, queen and husband where applicable...

The Man In The Glass

*Peter Dale Wimbrow Sr.*

When you get what you want in your struggle for self

And the world makes you king for a day

Just go to the mirror and look at yourself

And see what that man has to say.

For it isn't your father, or mother, or wife

Whose judgment upon you must pass

The fellow whose verdict counts most in your life

Is the one staring back from the glass.

He's the fellow to please – never mind all the rest

For he's with you, clear to the end

And you've passed your most difficult, dangerous test

If the man in the glass is your friend.

You may fool the whole world down the pathway of years

And get pats on the back as you pass

But your final reward will be heartache and tears

If you've cheated the man in the glass.

# Week 49

## TOUGH LOVE

At home and work let's keep in mind the dilemma of principles vs. procedures. Principles should always be known before procedures are asked to be followed. It's about how those principles are delivered, not just how procedures are explained. It's not about the rule being enforced, it's about how an individual enforces a rule. The manner in which we approach something can either curtail or derail a sensitive situation. Strategies & rules will always be in place but it's up to the individuals who enforce those rules to implement them in a fair manner. (In other words, it's not about the X's and the O's, it's about the Jimmy's and the Joe's)

Also, remember that tough love is necessary at times, but only when the person knows you love them. THE LOVE MUST COME FIRST OR THE TOUGH WON'T WORK!

# Week 50

> *"There are parts of a ship that which, taken by themselves, would sink. The engine would sink. The propeller would sink. But when the parts of a ship are built together, they float."*
>
> -Ralph W. Sockman

Finding unity among different types of people is one of life's greatest challenges. I consider myself blessed to have the team of people (faculty, staff and administrators) we have at my current school. We all bring our strengths to the building each day and because of that the building runs smoothly. Since mutual respect exists in our building nobody feels more worthy than the sum of everyone else. This proved to be very true and came to light during some recent events. Remember that it is not the position or rank that makes someone great, it is the person in the position that makes him or her great. Teamwork and selfless attitudes are what make our school tick.

In an email regarding help he received for an assembly he organized a staff member wrote: "I was truly overwhelmed by everyone's support and responsiveness. This is an example of many individual efforts coming together as one, and speaks to the cohesiveness and collaboration of our faculty and staff."

Nobody EXPECTED to be recognized for what they did. They assisted their colleagues because of their character, it's just who they are! So when in doubt or you need a helping hand, you should be able to turn to others in your building. Even though we all work in separate classrooms or offices, it doesn't mean we are divided in our goals.

*Week 51*

## DETACHMENT

When people use the word "detached" it usually takes on a negative meaning. To be detached means to be separate, disconnected, or lacking in emotional involvement. These are words that nobody wants to be associated with, unless you view yourself as a leader in your classroom or school. That's right... detachment can help you become a better leader! When we become attached too strongly to a belief or cause, our thinking tends to become skewed. To be detached as a leader helps to remove personal feelings from a situation without removing the "care" that needs to be there as well. Some people feel that when a decision does not go their way, that the decision-makers don't care. Students in your classes may feel that a decision is not fair but many are too immature to realize that some decisions are best for the group or may be best for the long term.

When making decisions at work or with your families we constantly need to detach to help clear our minds of emotion or personal feelings. When we detach we only need to do so for a brief moment in order to see the problem/solution clearly. Detaching yourself from an emotionally heated situation may be the only way to be IN the moment for the decision we have to make.

So ironically, the only way to "get a grip" is to DETACH…

# Week 52

Some thoughts on approaching each day with the right mindset:

1. Flexibility should not be interpreted as weakness just as Rigidity does not signify strength when dealing with people. A balance is needed.

2. Trust can be built by forgiving others, but abuse of that forgiveness requires communication or taking action.

3. Whatever you resist will persist, accept what is happening and learn from your decisions.

4. When you expect things to be a specific way, you may be setting yourself up for disappointment.

5. Welcoming change for what it is and people for who they are can limit stress.

6. Decisions will have to be made for the good of the group when working with others.

7.  Just like the branch of a tree

•   Bend but don't break

•   Recognize we are part of a greater whole

•   Go with the wind/flow

•   Extend yourself to reach your full potential